What is a man?
A man is nothing.
Without his family
He is of less importance
Than that bug
Crossing a trail.

Anonymous (Pomo), 1944

For Flying Turtle, Teacher, Coyote, and Friend.
CR

Library of Congress Cataloging-in-Publication Data

Dominic, Gloria, 1950-
    Coyote and the grasshoppers : a Pomo legend / by Gloria Dominic.
    p. cm. -- (Native American lore and legends)
    Includes index.
    Summary: By listening to the Great Spirit and eating huge quantities of grasshoppers. Coyote is able to save the Pomo from drought and starvation.
    ISBN 0-85593-427-4
    1. Pomo Indians--Folklore. 2. Tales--California.   [1. Pomo Indians--Folklore.
    2. Indians of North America--California--Folklore,
    3. Folklore--California.] I. Title. II. Series.
398.P6BD69   1998 • -- --
398.2'089'975--dc20   96-5114
                                             CIP
                                             AC

THE ROURKE CORPORATION, INC.

VERO BEACH, FLORIDA 32964

Designed by Susan and Dave Albers

■ NATIVE AMERICAN LORE & LEGENDS ■

COYOTE
AND THE
GRASSHOPPERS

A POMO LEGEND

ADAPTED AND RETOLD
BY GLORIA DOMINIC

ILLUSTRATED
BY CHARLES REASONER

This is a story of long ago. Once there was a sparkling lake. The Pomos who lived in the grassy hills nearby called it Clear Lake. From its crystal waters, the people fished and no one ever went hungry. In the waters of Clear Lake, the beauty of the wide sky of the Great Spirit was reflected for all to see.

But in time, a drought fell upon the land. Little by little, the waters of Clear Lake began to dry. The tasty fish died. The mud at the bottom of the lake turned to dust. Deep cracks, like the bare branches of trees, appeared where once the glittering water had shone.

The sun blazed day after day, and the Pomos grew hot and thirsty. Children cried for a drop of water to drink and a bite to eat. But there was no water. And there were no fish to eat. Birds and other animals became scarce. Plants withered, and there was not a berry to be found.

The Pomos gathered together. "What can we do to bring rain?" asked an elder. A wise old woman answered him, "We must ask the medicine men."

The medicine men did all they could. They sang chants to bring water to the land, but no rain came. The people gathered and danced for rain, but still none came.

One day, Coyote was roaming the dry land. As he searched for a bit of water to drink, he heard a sound. Bizzz-bizzz, bizzz-bizzz!

Coyote looked up and could not believe his eyes. A large cloud was moving across the land. "What is this strange sight?" he wondered.

As the cloud moved closer, Coyote saw it was a swarming mass of grasshoppers, too many to count! The chirping of the grasshoppers filled Coyote's ears with a loud bizzing noise.

Coyote watched as the grasshoppers ate everything in their path. Each blade of grass disappeared as the insects passed over the hills. This made things even worse for the Pomos. Without the seeds from the grass, the people could not make the thick mush that was now their only food.

Coyote could not understand why these terrible things were happening. "I will ask the Great Spirit what to do," he said. "Perhaps there is a way to help the Pomos—and to get a bit of water for myself!"

Coyote threw back his head to howl. But his throat was so parched and dry, he could only make a small, rasping sound. Still, the Great Spirit answered him. "Why do you call me?" he asked.

"Times are hard for the Pomos and for all creatures," said Coyote. "Our lakes are dry. Our food is scarce. And now, to make things worse, ugly grasshoppers are eating everything in sight. We must bring water back to Clear Lake."

"I will tell you what to do," said the Great Spirit. "If you are hungry, eat your fill of grasshoppers. Then all else will follow."

Coyote did not like this advice. "Eat grasshoppers!" he said. "They do not look very tasty."

"All creatures are on earth for a reason," said the Great Spirit. "You will discover the reason for grasshoppers if you do as I say."

Reluctantly, Coyote trotted off among the insects. "I hope Great Spirit is right," he grumbled. He quickly snapped his head back and forth among the grasshoppers, catching great mouthfuls of them. Gulp, gulp! Down his throat they went.

Although the grasshoppers jumped about and tickled his throat, Coyote had to admit that they were quite filling. He continued to run over the hills, gobbling as many of the insects as he could.

Finally, Coyote couldn't eat another bite. He lay down on his back to rest. His stomach was swollen with the huge meal he'd just eaten.

Then Coyote heard a voice. It was the Great Spirit. "Why have you stopped eating? There are still many grasshoppers left."

"I am so full, there is no room for a single grasshopper!" moaned Coyote.

"Nonsense," said the Great Spirit. "Do you want to help the Pomos?"

"Yes," said Coyote.

"Then eat!" answered the Great Spirit.

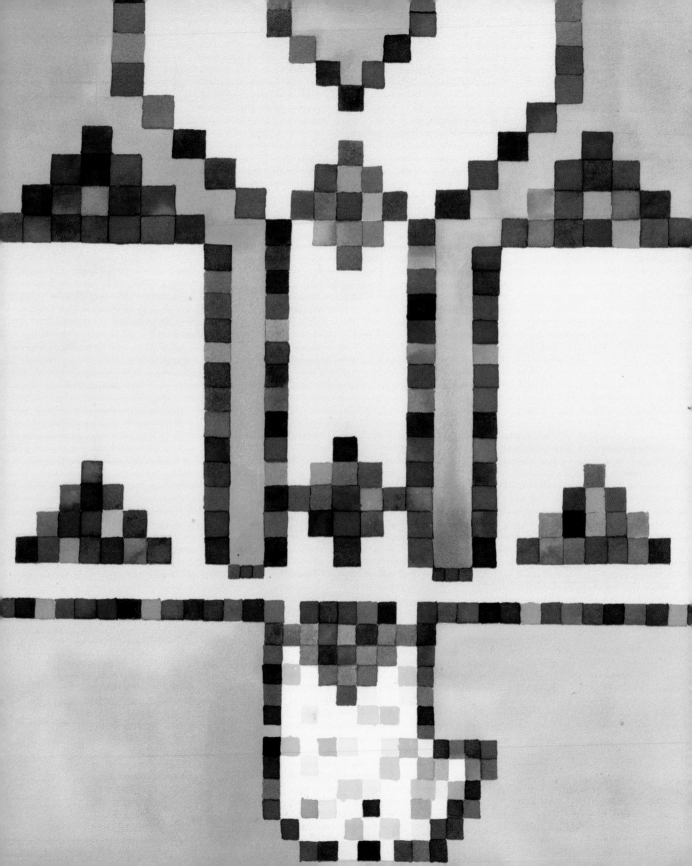

oyote pulled himself to his feet. Again, he trotted off among the grasshoppers, eating all he could. The only way he could force another down his throat was to think of the hungry Pomo children. He knew fewer grasshoppers meant there would be more grass for the Pomos' mush.

At last Coyote could eat no more. "Great Spirit," he called, "I've eaten almost all the grasshoppers. But I will burst if I eat the few that are left."

"Do not worry," said the Great Spirit. "You have done well. But I have another task for you."

Coyote yowled in disbelief. He was so full, he could hardly move. How could he possibly perform another task?

"Do you see the grasshoppers that you have not eaten?" asked the Great Spirit.

Coyote nodded.

"Follow them," said the Great Spirit.

Coyote was so full, it was hard for him to get up. Finally, he managed to sit. The last of the grasshoppers were moving in a line across the hills. With a weary moan, Coyote struggled to stand. But he could not.

Again the Great Spirit spoke. "Think of the hungry children."

Coyote did. The thought gave him the strength to stand. He set off after the grasshoppers. To his surprise, they led him straight to the patch of dry dirt that used to be Clear Lake.

Weary and still too full, Coyote was about to sink into a heap
and take a long nap. Then he heard a small sound.
Gurgle, gurgle. Coyote knew that sound. Could it be?

20

Yes! In the middle of the dry earth that was once a lake, Coyote saw a tiny spring. The little bit of water made a happy sound as it bubbled out of the ground.

Then Coyote heard a familiar voice. "Do not stop now," said the Great Spirit. "You have work to do, if you are to help the Pomos. Dig as deeply as you can at the spring."

"I cannot," said Coyote. "I am too full."

"Dig!" urged the Great Spirit.

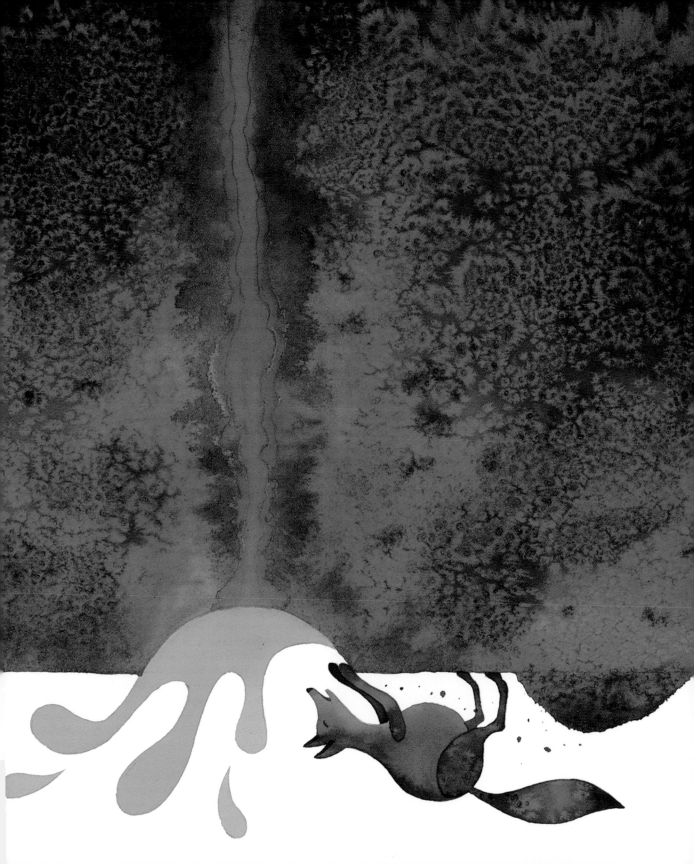

Coyote slowly dragged himself to the spring. He took a small sip. The water tasted so sweet! Then he began to dig. He dug and dug and dug. The deeper he dug, the more water came out of the ground. It ran swiftly from the hole Coyote made, rushing and swirling to fill the bed of the lake.

When at last the water stopped running, Coyote looked out upon a beautiful lake. Tired as he was, he ran to the villages of the Pomos, yowling and howling as loudly as he could.

The villagers ran out of their huts when they heard all the noise. Coyote continued to howl. "Come see the lake," Coyote cried. "Come drink the sweet, clear water!" But the people did not understand what he was trying to tell them.

The wise men and wise women gathered. "What is the matter with Coyote?" they asked one another. "Perhaps he has gone mad with thirst," suggested one.

"He is only begging for food," said another.

But a small child saw the fullness of Coyote's belly and knew the animal could not be hungry. He listened again to the loud howling. Then the boy thought he heard the Great Spirit whispering in his ear.

"I know why Coyote is howling," the child said. "He says the water has come back to Clear Lake."

The Pomos ran excitedly to the lake. Coyote bounded along beside them. From the top of a hill, the people stopped and stared. The little boy's words were true! The waters of Clear Lake shimmered in the sunlight.

The people drank and quenched their thirst. Coyote's heart was full of happiness at the sight. But then he heard a bizzing sound. The grasshoppers! In his excitement, Coyote had forgotten all about the few remaining insects.

Again, Coyote heard the voice of the Great Spirit. "I told you that all creatures have a purpose. Now you will find out the reason for grasshoppers. Chase the last of the grasshoppers into the lake."

Coyote did as he was told. Yapping and snapping, he ran after the insects. The people watched in amazement. They had never seen Coyote act this way before.

The grasshoppers jumped nearer and nearer to the water to escape Coyote's snapping jaws. Then, bizzing and buzzing, they hopped into Clear Lake. As they did, each grasshopper became a shining silvery fish! Away the fish swam, darting through the beautiful water.

Now the people cheered. "The fish are back in Clear Lake," they cried. "We will not go hungry!"

Coyote let out a one final happy howl. At last, he understood the words of the Great Spirit. He also learned that a heart that is strong and unselfish can help others.

To this day, the Pomos remember the time of the drought. They tell the story of how brave Coyote brought water and bountiful fish back to Clear Lake. That is why the Pomos love Coyote!

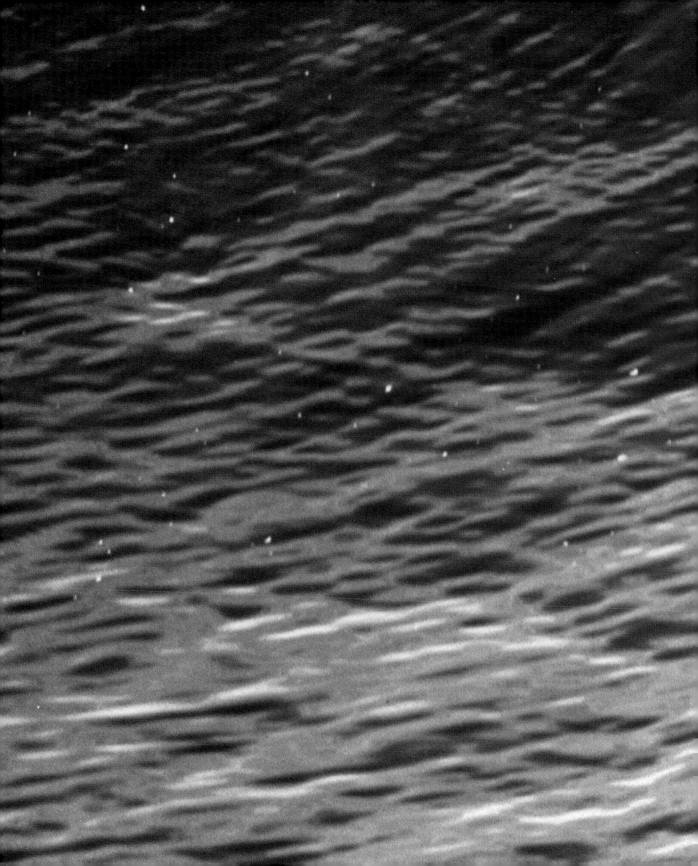

The Pomo

Above. A hut made from one of the species of tule, which was too thick for finely woven baskets.

THE POMO

Pomo Homeland

The Pomo homeland was north of San Francisco Bay, across Central California in what is now Sonoma, Mendocino, and Lake Counties. Although some lived along the Pacific Coast separated from other Pomos by giant Redwood forests, most lived inland—in the sunny areas along the Russian River and around Clear Lake.

Depending on where they lived, their homes were either round or rectangular huts, covered with bark, grass, or tule (tall plants). Tule is a reed like plant that grows near water. These huts could house one or many related families. Villages were made up of related families with a hereditary headsman or headswoman—two, if the village was large. All villages had a sweat lodge where men met and slept. It was dug into the ground and covered with earth. Women and children slept in the huts, which were also used for cooking and storage. These homes were only for winter use. In summer, mats supported by poles or brush was enough for shelter. Large villages also had a "singing lodge," a larger structure made of earth and grass for councils and ceremonies. Families lived in the same area and harvested from the same oak trees generation after generation.

Pomo People

The Pomo were made up of many small groups of people who spoke seven related languages. Like some Californian tribes, the Pomo were hunter-gathers. Men fished, trapped, and hunted. They also built homes, traps, and tools. Women wandered over large areas, gathering food. They also prepared food, made clothing, and raised children, who also helped gather food.

Pomos were known for their exquisite baskets. Baskets were used as traps, tools, cradles, gifts, and storage containers. They were also traded for tools, weapons, shells, and furs. Both sexes were accomplished basket weavers. They used a variety of techniques and intricate patterns. Most baskets had thirty wrappings to an inch, but Pomo baskets often had sixty or

Above. A sample of Pomo money. The Pomo men were the major manufacturers of this form of money, for their tribe as well as for many other California tribes.

Right and center. A Pomo family homeward bound with their baskets. These baskets were used to carry roots, and the spaces in the open weave allowed dirt to fall through.

more. Gift baskets were richly decorated with beads, shells, and tiny colorful feathers.

The Pomo also made money that was used by other Californian natives. Shells were broken into small rounded beads and strung in groups. Using these strings, Pomos were able to count into the tens of thousands. Some groups also mined a mineral called magnesite which was baked and polished until they turned beautiful colors, like reds and pinks. These were very valuable and treated like jewels.

Left. One of the many ornate baskets that the Pomo are known for creating.

Food and Clothing

Men wore loincloths or no clothing in summer. Women wore skirts made of fibers from bark, grass, tule, or occasionally, deerskin. They also sometimes wore capes that hung to the skirts. Both went barefoot, but some groups wore skin moccasins for walking in snow. In winter, both wore furs or fiber blankets for warmth.

Food came from many sources: birds, fish, and seafood from the ocean, lakes, and rivers; berries, seeds, and roots from wild plants; small game from the forest; and acorns from the mighty oak tree. Acorns were nutritious, plentiful, and easy to store. But it took hard work before they could be eaten. Men and boys climbed trees and shook branches, or used poles to knock down acorns. Women and children gathered and shelled them. They were ground into flour by stone pestles and mortars. Water was gently poured over the flour many times to wash away the bitter acid. Then the flour was mixed with clean water. Hot rocks were dropped into the mixture to cook it into mush. Mush was eaten alone, mixed with berries, or molded into a cake and baked. Acorns were stored in large baskets in the home for one family, or in huge baskets kept above ground on poles for several families.

Top. Acorn storage caches like these were used to store acorns until they were ready to grind them into flour.

Bottom. A Pomo woman carrying her child in a tule papoose.

Top. A Pomo family dressed in their Sunday best.

Left. A muli-colored Pomo basket completely covered with shells.

Bottom. A basket weaver using one of the many different ways to make a basket.

Top. In 1900, the upper lake Pomo people posed in front of the Frank Howe General Store.

Pomo Today

Today Pomo people live in cities and towns such as Ukiah and Santa Rosa, California with non-natives, and on small rancherias instead of on large reservations.

While some have become teachers, writers, and fire fighters, many still work recreating traditional crafts and ways, such as basket making or practicing of Pomo medicine.

Bottom. Pomo fire dancers in 1912 dressed for a spiritual ceremony.

Top. Dancers wearing hats made with feathers.

Bottom. A boat made of tule in 1900. These boats easily became waterlogged and they were brought to shore to dry out.

Right. A single tule hut.

Glossary

Acorn: The nut-like seed of oak trees

Magnesite: A light-colored mineral

Maru: A dreamer whose visions and teachings inspires religious rituals and guides the religious life of the community. Also the name of the religion

Rancherias: Areas set aside for natives to live, usually smaller than reservations

Sedge: A grass-like plant that the Pomo used for basket weaving

Sweat lodge: A structure where men met to talk, sweat, and sleep

Tule: A tall plant with stiff stems that is only found near water

Right. A grouping of beautiful Pomo baskets. The Pomo were the experts and used a wider variety of techniques than any other tribe near them.

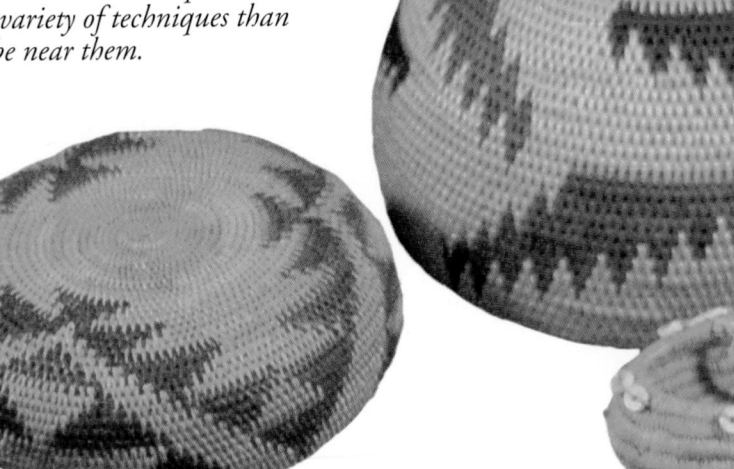

43

Important Dates

1492: Columbus lands in the Americas.

1542: Spanish explorer Juan Rodrigues Cabrillo lands along the Pacific Coast.

1741: Russian surveyor Vitus Bering surveys Bering Sea for Russia.

1812: Russian trading post, Fort Ross, established in Pomo country.

1846 - 1848: Mexican War between the United States and Mexico.

1848: The Treaty of Guadalupe Hidalgo ends the Mexican War. As part of the agreement, Mexico cedes California to the United States.

Above. A tule boat that was in the 4th of July parade for the Lake County Centennial.

1849: California Gold Rush.

1850: California becomes the 31st state.

1924: All Native Americans born in the U.S. declared citizens.

1968: Indian Civil Rights Act gives Native Americans the right to govern themselves on their reservations.

Above. Basket weavers, such as this Pomo woman, put many hours into making their beautiful baskets.

Top left and bottom right. Baskets displaying some of the different patterns and colors used by the Pomo.

PHOTO CREDITS

We want to extend a special thank you to Cindy Drummond, from the Lake County Museum, Lakeport, CA, for all of her help in acquiring images for this book.

Pages 32-33: Water, Photo by Dave Albers
Pomo woman gathering tule, Courtesy of the Lake County Museum, Lakeport, CA

Pages 34-35: Map by Dave Albers
Tule hut, Courtesy of the Lake County Museum, Lakeport, CA

Pages 36-37: Shell money and basket, Photos by Cindy Drummond
Pomos carrying baskets, Courtesy of the Lake County Museum, Lakeport, CA

Pages 38-39: Acorn storage cache, Courtesy of the Lake County Museum, Lakeport, CA
Pomo women and their children, Courtesy of the Lake County Museum, Lakeport, CA
Basket, Photo by Cindy Drummond

Pages 40-41: All images Courtesy of the Lake County Museum, Lakeport, CA

Pages 42-43: Dancers, tule boat, and tule hut Courtesy of the Lake County Museum, Lakeport, CA
Baskets, Photos by Cindy Drummond

Pages 44-45: Baskets, Photos by Cindy Drummond
Parade float and basket weaver, Courtesy of the Lake County Museum, Lakeport, CA

Pages 47-48: Pomo woman, Courtesy of the Lake County Museum, Lakeport, CA
Basket, Photo by Cindy Drummond
Basket, Dover Books

POMO BIBLIOGRAPHY

Bauer, Helen. California Indian Days. Garden City, NY: Doubleday & Co., 1963.

Boule, Mary Null. Western and Northeastern Pomo Tribes. Vashon, WA: Merryant Publishing, 1992.

Brown, Vinson and Douglas Andrews. The Pomo Indians of California and Their Neighbors. Happy Camp, CA: Naturegraph Publishers, 1969.

Editors of Time-Life Books. The American Indians: The Woman's Way. Alexandria, VA: Time-Life Books, 1995.

Emanuels, George. California Indians. Walnut Creek, CA: George Emanuels dba Diablo Books, 1990.

Heizer, R.F. and M.A. Whipple. The California Indians: A Source Book. Berkeley, CA: The University of California Press, 1971.

Kroeber, A.L. Handbook of the Indians of California. New York: Dover Publications, 1976.

Maxwell, James A., Editor. America's Fascinating Indian Heritage. Pleasantville, NY: Reader's Digest Association, 1978.

Sturtevant, William C., General Editor. Handbook of North American Indians: California (Volume 8). Washington: Smithsonian Institution, 1978.

Waldman, Carl. Encyclopedia of North American Tribes. New York: Facts on File, 1988.

Worthylake, Mary M. The Pomo. Chicago: Children's Press, 1994.

Above. A Pomo from Long Valley. She is between 110 and 120 years old.

Right. A Pomo basket adorned with shells.

SECOND NATURE

CHANGES & CHALLENGES IN THE NEW ENVIRONMENT

All photos courtesy of Getty Images, except for the following:
Black Book Partners (16, 18, 26); Associated Press (22); Deposit Photos (24, 27); Panama
Amphibian Rescue and Conservation Project (28), State of Utah Department of Natural
Resources (33); Kirk Johnson (34); Rebecca Noblin (43); Peter Clark, Tampa Bay Watch (44).

Front Cover: Peter Clark, Tampa Bay Watch

Special thanks to Content Consultant Ashley McDowell.

Library of Congress Cataloging-in-Publication Data

Tilmont, Amy.
  Man vs. animal : species at risk / by Amy Tilmont, Jeff Garside, Mark
Stewart.
      p. cm.
  Includes bibliographical references and index.
  Summary: "This book takes young readers deep into the complicated and
often destructive relationship between humans and nature. Man vs. Animal
brings into sharp focus issues that include habitat destruction, climate
change, land management and introduction of invasive species--while offering
actionable solutions for each both now and in the future"--Provided by
publisher.
  ISBN-13: 978-1-59953-460-2 (library edition : alk. paper)
  ISBN-10: 1-59953-460-6 (library edition : alk. paper)
1. Nature--Effect of human beings on--Juvenile literature. 2.
Environmental degradation--Juvenile literature. 3. Human-animal
relationships--Juvenile literature. I. Garside, Jeff. II. Stewart, Mark,
1960- III. Title.
  GF75.T55 2012
  304.2--dc23
                            2011017630

Manufactured in the United States of America in North Mankato, Minnesota.
176N—072011

COVER: A brown pelican watches as an oil fire rages in the waters off the Florida coast. Animals are often put in danger by human activity.

The world's population will probably reach 10 billion in your lifetime. All those people will need places to live, food to eat, and water to drink. That is not good news for the animal species—which include humans, of course—that compete for the same resources. Add to this the stresses of air and water pollution, and changing **ecosystems** due to **climate change**, and Man vs. Animal doesn't look like a very fair fight.

People tend to think of the "battles" between humans and animals as taking place far away. But the fact is that we put species at risk in our own communities—sometimes even in our own backyards—every day. In some cases, the damage we do is slow and occurs over time. Rarely do we see a single event that snaps us to attention and makes us wonder aloud, "Have we gone too far?"

OIL IN THE GULF

One such event was the ecological disaster in the Gulf of Mexico during the spring and summer of 2010. It was called an "oil leak," but that did not begin to describe what

Human activity has threatened the Siberian tiger population. Now humans must bring it back from the brink.

An egret looks for food on the oily shores of the Gulf of Mexico.

was happening. An accident on an off-shore oil-drilling platform damaged the pipe bringing oil to the surface. The break occurred more than 3,000 feet (914.4 meters) deep, or about 1 mile (1.6 kilometers). No one had a plan to repair the damage because everyone assumed the platform's safety systems would prevent a "blowout." In fact, no one even knew who was in charge of fixing the problem or cleaning up the mess. By the time the well was capped, around 200 million gallons (757 million liters) of oil had entered the Gulf's delicate ecosystem.

People all over the world watched on television as the oil slick reached the wetlands and beaches of five southern states. They saw pictures on the Internet of dead and dying wildlife. They listened to environmental scientists guess what the short-term and long-term damage might be.

People who live and work in the region depend on clean water and beaches. No one could tell them when their lives would return to normal. Meanwhile, everyone wondered how this could have happened in the first place.

The Gulf oil disaster focused attention on the threat humans pose to animals because of pollution. People pollute the environment in many different ways. For example, **fertilizing** a lawn or throwing away old computers could do great harm. This doesn't mean you should stop taking care of your yard or keep old computers forever. It is simply a reminder that all of our actions have consequences in the natural world. In other words, we have to think before we act.

Where were the scientists?

Balancing the energy needs of people against the safety of ecosystems is not an easy job. Making a good plan takes ideas from all sides, including environmental scientists. Unfortunately, they are not always invited to contribute. The decisions about safety and procedures that led to the 2010 Gulf oil disaster were made by people in business and politics. Would things have turned out differently if scientists had a strong voice?

No one can say for sure. However, the world learned two important lessons. First, what's good for business often is not good for animal species. Second, and more important, what's bad for animal species is almost always bad for business. The Gulf economy may never recover from the loss of jobs in fishing and tourism, and the marine and wetland ecosystems may never be the same.

Believe it or not, there is a far greater threat to animal species than the millions of gallons of oil leaked into the Gulf of Mexico. It is air pollution. The **greenhouse gases** emitted from homes, businesses, and automobiles are changing the earth's atmosphere. The planet appears to be getting warmer—no one can agree how much or how fast temperatures will change, but everyone agrees that any change is bad for animals.

The way that animals breed and eat and live corresponds very closely to their surrounding environment. Some become very specialized. A small change in temperature or in the food chain can have disastrous consequences for them. As the climate changes and ecosystems are disrupted, countless species around the planet are pushed closer and closer to the edge of extinction.

HABITAT DESTRUCTION

Climate change and habitat destruction often go hand in hand. In recent years, the plight of the polar bear has made headlines. Polar bears travel and hunt across great sheets of ice. Warming temperatures in the Arctic have broken up these ice sheets and reduced their size, threatening this habitat. Heartbreaking photos and videos show confused and exhausted bears trying to survive.

Little can be done to reverse climate change immediately, so the United States government did the next best thing. It listed polar bears as a protected species in 2008 and set

Climate changes are melting many of the regions where polar bears live. They also face threats in Alaska where energy companies do business.

aside more than 100 million acres of coastal land in Alaska as critical habitat in 2010. Did that solve the problem? Not exactly.

Polar bears will be at risk until more work is done to fix the larger problem of **emissions** of **carbon dioxide** into the atmosphere. They also face another challenge. This one comes from energy companies drilling for oil in Alaska. They do not think the bears should be protected. Drilling for oil in the habitats of protected species is difficult and expensive. Companies are required to show that their activities will not harm the area. In 2011, some energy companies sued the government to take polar bears off the protected list. The fate of this species may be decided in court!

SEA HUNT

A problem that has become a major issue in the world's oceans is fishing. Several species that were once abundant have been "overfished," and scientists worry that it will take many years to rebuild their populations. In recent years, overfishing has sent the world's population of tuna into steep decline.

Tuna are like the fighter jets of the ocean. They are fast, powerful killing machines that feed on other fish, squid, and shellfish. Because tuna are big and muscular, they are a favorite on the dinner table in almost every culture in the world. In 1950, **commercial fishermen** hauled in 600,000 tons (544 million kilograms) of tuna. This may seem like a lot, but it barely affected the tuna population. Today, that number is 10 times larger—and fishermen still cannot keep up with world demand.

Scientists estimate that Atlantic bluefin populations are down between 70 and 90 percent since 1950.

In 2009, the European Union considered a fishing ban on a tuna known as the Atlantic bluefin. Scientists estimated that it might disappear from its breeding grounds in the Mediterranean Sea within a few years. The ban was voted down and fishing continued.

Eventually, there will be so few tuna that it won't be worth trying to catch them anymore. Perhaps that is what needs to happen for their populations to recover. Unfortunately, it isn't that simple. Tuna are top predators in their ecosystems. When a top predator disappears, no one can be sure what will take its place or what the consequences will be. Given how little we understand about the food chain in the open ocean, it is impossible to predict what might happen next.

WORLD VIEW

What does it mean if a species is endangered? Its numbers are so low that it's on the brink of extinction. There are hundreds of mammals on the list of endangered species. They come in all shapes and sizes and from all parts of the world. As the map below shows, that may include your own backyard!

Endangered Mammals

1	Asian Elephant	Sri Lanka
2	Bison	Plains of the United States
3	Black Rhino	Namibia
4	Cheetah	Iran
5	Giant Panda	China
6	Gray Wolf	Canada
7	Grevy's Zebra	Kenya
8	Grizzly Bear	Alaska
9	Humpback Whale	Arctic Ocean
10	Manatee	Cuba
11	Polar Bear	Greenland
12	Red Panda	Nepal
13	Tiger	India

NOTE: Data compiled by ThinkQuest.org

2 Got Here

OUR CONQUEST OF ANIMALS

When people and animals compete for land and resources, animals don't stand much of a chance. When animals *become* a resource, they face the very real prospect of extinction. Time and again throughout history, species hunted for their meat or commercial value have seen their populations crash. By the time **conservation** scientists are invited into the picture, it is often too late.

The "battle" between people and animals was not always so one-sided. Indeed, before the invention of effective hunting tools and techniques, humans were just as likely to be on the dinner menu as the creatures they hunted. The balance began to tilt around 30,000 years ago, during the Upper Paleolithic period. Hunters became skilled at making and using weapons such as spears and arrows, which could kill animals at a distance. Humans could finally compete with nature's top predators.

Large mammals provided food for early humans. Today, these species face new threats, including being kept in captivity like these elephants.

Dead as a Dodo

Sometimes, humans can wipe out an entire species without even realizing it. In the 1600s, the Dodo (right) went extinct shortly after European settlers arrived on the island of Mauritius, off the coast of Africa in the Indian Ocean. The Dodo was a large, flightless bird. Its meat did not taste good, so it was not hunted for food. At least, it wasn't hunted by people.

When Europeans arrived in the late 1500s, they brought pigs with them. The pigs were a primary source of food. Because Mauritius was covered with crabs, the settlers also brought crab-eating Macaque monkeys from the Philippines. Within 100 years, the Dodo was extinct. There had been some habitat destruction and human hunting, but it was the invasive species that doomed the Dodo. The pigs and monkeys brought to Mauritius **plundered** Dodo eggs and chicks until the population crashed.

Where humans lived, those other predators began to disappear and eventually died out. They could not compete with people for large prey animals. When humans replaced top predators—including cave lions, dire wolves, and saber-toothed cats—it threw ecosystems wildly out of balance. Large mammals could not reproduce fast enough to survive. In North America, for example, ground sloths, mammoths, mastodons, and early forms of horses and camels went extinct within a few thousand years of man's arrival. The combination of ecosystem destruction and overhunting still poses a threat to species all over the world.

BRINK OF EXTINCTION

More recently, other animals have been pushed to the brink of extinction by humans. Commercial hunters—people who hunt for a living—operate according to a simple equation. The more they kill, the more money they make. During the 1500s and 1600s in Europe, beaver pelts were in great demand by makers of hats and clothes. The animal was hunted to extinction. The North American beaver might have suffered the same fate in the 1700s and 1800s, but luckily beaver fur went out of style.

For nearly four centuries beginning in the 1600s, the world's whale population came under enormous stress from commercial hunting. The high demand for meat and oil in Europe (and later in America) made it worthwhile to create organized whaling fleets. People ate whale meat and used the animal's oil for lamps in the days before gas and electricity.

In the 1800s, during the early days of the Industrial Revolution, demand for whale oil soared. It was needed to keep machines running smoothly. It was also used

This print from the 1800s shows how whaling fleets
used to hunt in the seas.

for making fabrics, paint, and margarine. Several species
of whale were hunted to the brink of extinction.

It was not until the 1930s that countries agreed to
limit their catches—and not until the 1980s that whaling
was strictly limited. What "saved" the whales was not
mankind's concern for their survival, however. It was
the discovery of petroleum under the ground, which was
cheaper than whale oil.

Can a species be too big to fail? *No.* People who defended whaling claimed it would be impossible to wipe out whale populations. There were just far too many animals in the world's ocean for that to happen. The same thing was said of the passenger pigeon, which was one of the most common birds in North America during the 1700s and 1800s. Passenger flocks were so large that they could blot out the sun when they flew overhead. One flock was measured at a mile wide and 300 miles (483 kilometers) long!

Passenger pigeons nested in huge colonies consisting of hundreds of thousands of birds. This helped protect them against predators. It also made them easy to hunt on a large scale. In the United States, slave owners bought low-priced pigeon meat to feed to their slaves. Poor people in the North ate the same meat as well. At the same time, vast forests were being cut down to build towns and cities. Passenger pigeons had fewer and fewer places to nest. When European settlers arrived in North America, there were as many as 5 billion passenger pigeons. By the early 1900s, there were just a handful. Martha, the last passenger pigeon, died in 1914 at the Cincinnati Zoo.

When a rainforest is leveled, the species living
there must find a new habitat.

VANISHING RAINFORESTS

During the past 100 years, habitat loss and pollution
have surpassed hunting in most areas as the greatest threat to
animals. The plight of the world's rainforests helps explain
why this has happened. Rainforests are cleared for timber,
agriculture, mineral resources, and human habitation. In
poor countries, this has made them an important source
of income for people and businesses. But every square mile
of rainforest that disappears pushes a species or two that
much closer to extinction.

In the 1960s, oil was discovered beneath Ecuador's
remote eastern rainforest. Soon thousands of people were

living and working in this fragile ecosystem. The damage caused to animals by this activity was considerable. However, many felt the region would recover once the oil had been removed. What they did not account for was the pollution produced by the drilling.

More than 30 billion gallons (114 billion liters) of oil and toxic chemicals leaked or were dumped into the surrounding environment. Hundreds of square miles were polluted. In some places, no plants could grow, and no fish could live. The animal species that depend on these food sources suffered greatly, too. But what finally drew attention to this problem was the effect the pollution had on the people living in this part of Ecuador. Many developed cancer and other diseases. Children were born with terrible birth defects. Animals were given a better chance to survive only after humans were put in danger.

VISITING THE ZOO

The place where most people come face-to-face with animals is a zoo. The word is short for Zoological Park or Zoological Garden—the old-time names for the places where animals were collected and studied by scientists. Now some zoos are called bioparks or wildlife conservation parks.

The first zoos opened during the 1700s in Austria, Spain, and France. They looked a little bit like jails for animals. As scientists came to understand animals better, they began designing zoos to feel more like natural habitats. The first zoo to do so was in Germany during the early 1900s. Since the 1970s, most zoos have tried to do the same. Studying animals in these environments makes it easier for researchers to understand their behavior. This knowledge helps efforts to conserve species at risk.

3 If We Do Nothing
THE THREAT OF EXTINCTION

We know from fossil records that life on earth rises and falls. Sometimes it thrives, and sometimes it struggles. Science recognizes five great extinction events in earth's history. During these times, there was a sharp drop in the number of larger life forms on the planet. With each event, life on earth was dramatically reshaped. The fifth (and last) major extinction event occurred 65 million years ago. In the aftermath, mammals rose to take the place of dinosaurs as the dominant species on earth.

Some believe that we are in the midst of the sixth great extinction. Typically, between 10 and 100 species go extinct each year—from the largest plants and animals to the tiniest organisms. This is called the "background level" of extinction. Right now we may be losing more than 10,000 species a year. If we do nothing, scientists estimate that half of the world's plant and animal species may cease to exist by the end of this century.

A museum worker tends to a life-sized replica of a woolly mammoth and its baby. These great creatures used to roam North America.

A honeybee
pollinates a flower.

We tend to focus on large animals when we think of extinction. But fewer than 100 species of mammals have gone extinct over the past 400 years. There are still roughly 5,000 species of mammals on the planet. Most of the species that humans have pushed to the brink are barely noticeable—and have barely been studied. Often we do not understand the role they play in their ecosystems. We have even less understanding of how those ecosystems will react once those species are gone. What if one of those species holds the clues to curing a disease such as cancer? In the battle between man and animal, humans may be the short-term "winners." In the long run, however, we may be the biggest losers of all.

DISAPPEARING BEES

Bees may be small creatures, but they provide huge benefits to humans. For example, farmers depend on bees to pollinate their crops. As bees move from flower to flower, they transfer pollen that enables the plants to reproduce and grow. If bees don't do their jobs—or if there aren't enough bees to get the job done—the result could be a severe food shortage.

In 2006, beekeepers noticed that entire hives of honeybees were dying overnight. No one knew exactly why this was happening. Was it a virus? Was there something else going on? The problem was given a serious name: Colony Collapse Disorder (CCD). The United States Department of Agriculture put together a team of scientists to investigate this mystery.

What made their research difficult was that the bees weren't dying in their hives. They would fly away in search of pollen and never return. Each year the problem got worse. In 2010, 34 percent of American hives were affected by CCD. The prime "suspects" were **pesticides**, **parasites**, a **fungus**, or a virus. Or perhaps it was a combination. Or maybe one triggered another.

Unfortunately, as of 2011, there were still no clear answers to this problem. If nothing is done, eventually more than 130 different crops will suffer. Those crops are worth more than $15 billion a year. They feeds thousands and thousands of people.

GENETIC CHANGES

Many scientists believe that the earth's warming climate has begun to create genetic changes in several animal species. In other words, some animals may survive by evolving—right before our very eyes! Canadian biologists studying the North American red squirrel noticed that certain squirrels were breeding a few days earlier each year. Rising temperatures where the red squirrel lives in the Yukon Territory caused spruce trees to bloom earlier. The squirrels born earlier in the spring survive better than the ones born later. Scientists are watching carefully to see if they evolve into a different species.

This button celebrates the accomplishments of Lewis and Clark. Their exploration included the Crown of the Continent.

CROWN OF THE CONTINENT

Environmental scientists study all kinds of ecosystems, from very small to very large. One they are watching carefully is located on 10 million mountainous acres in western Montana and the Canadian provinces of Alberta and British Columbia. Meriwether Lewis and William Clark explored these areas in the early 1800s during their famous expedition from the Mississippi River to the Pacific Ocean. Later in that century, a naturalist named George Grinnell called this region the Crown of the Continent.

Why does the Crown of the Continent fascinate researchers? Not a single animal that lived there when Lewis and Clark first trekked through the area has gone extinct. And there are a lot of animals in the region. In fact, only a handful of places in the world can claim greater **biodiversity**. That makes the Crown's ecosystem a "laboratory" for watching the effects of climate change—now the greatest threat to animals in their relationship with humans.

The glaciers that feed the life-giving rivers and streams in the Crown are melting at a rate of almost 100 feet each year.

SNAKES IN THE 'GLADES

Sometimes our love of animals "backfires" and actually threatens entire ecosystems. Each year thousands of Americans buy Burmese pythons (right) as pets. When these snakes grow too large or become too expensive to feed, loving owners set them free. In the Florida Everglades, the population of Burmese pythons has exploded. In Asia, the pythons are in balance with other predators, and their numbers are small. In the Everglades, they are the top predators.

Scientists worry because Burmese pythons are good hunters and fast breeders. In the Everglades, they have begun to prey on endangered species living in the area, including other predatory snakes that had kept the environment in balance for thousands of years. The problem was made worse when a breeding facility was damaged during a hurricane and the snakes escaped. Now Florida employs snake hunters to capture and destroy Burmese pythons. These hunters are the last line of defense for dozens of native species.

Snow in many areas is melting a month earlier than in the past. This is a problem for creatures such as the snowshoe hare, whose fur turns bright white in the winter. A white rabbit moving on brown or green ground is an easy target for predators. So far the snowshoe hare and other specialized animals are managing to survive. We are seeing that nature can be very persistent. But how long can this ecosystem hold up? Unfortunately, we may have the answer sooner rather than later.

4 Bright Ideas

FINDING COMMON GROUND WITH ANIMALS

Many smart and talented people are looking for ways to strike a balance between the needs of humans and the survival of animal species. Together, they make up a small but dedicated army. Their victories take place in remote jungles, university laboratories, and courtrooms. Their goal is not to turn back the clock—they know this is impossible. Rather, they are trying to find workable solutions while there is still time.

One of the most urgent problems is the world's frog population. Frogs are very sensitive to changes in the surrounding environment. When scientists see frog populations fall, they know something is wrong. Several years ago, research showed that one-third of frog species was crashing. The culprit was identified as the chytrid fungus, which grows in wet environments. It causes chytridiomycosis, a condition that is fatal to frogs. The disease was first identified in African frogs many decades ago. It spread globally through frogs that were sold for medical testing, food, and exotic pets.

Saving frog populations is a goal of many environmental scientists, including those at the Panama Amphibian Rescue and Conservation Project.

In 2009, eight major conservation organizations, including several large zoos, put together the Amphibian Rescue and Conservation Project. They set up a lab in Panama, which has one of the world's largest amphibian populations—including at least 50 species that are endangered or at risk. Their work could have a huge impact on frogs, and they may learn things that benefit humans, too.

WHY FROGS ARE IMPORTANT

Frogs **secrete** chemicals that do remarkable things. For example, these secretions protect their skin and help them communicate. Not surprisingly, medical researchers have become very interested in this topic. Testing shows that frog secretions may help us develop new drugs that fight diseases such as cancer and viruses that include **human immunodeficiency virus (HIV)**. Losing just one frog species could be a matter of life and death for humans.

SAVING OYSTERS

Of course, not all animals that need the attention or protection of science are cute or furry. That doesn't mean they deserve any less attention. During the 1900s, the species of oyster native to the Chesapeake Bay (*Crassostrea virginica*) went into a steep decline. Centuries earlier, there were billions of oysters in the bay. By 2000, about 99 percent were gone—pollution, disease, and **overharvesting** were the main causes. Several attempts to restore the oysters had failed.

In 2004, a team of researchers from the Virginia Institute of Marine Science at the College of William & Mary tried something different. They created an artificial reef near

Scientists study oyster samples from the Great Wicomico River. Their work has enabled this species to make a comeback.

the mouth of the Great Wicomico River. They built the reef higher in the water than others had tried. This bright idea kept the young oysters from being choked by thick bottom **sediment**. Now there are more than 200,000 healthy oysters living on the reef. Plans are in place to build many more "oyster sanctuaries" in the Chesapeake Bay.

The people who fish the bay could not be happier with the results. They know what marine scientists do—a healthy oyster population filters the water, creates places for other organisms to live, and makes for great fish habitats.

PRESERVING LAND

Bright ideas can be expensive sometimes. Funding projects such as the Panama Amphibian Rescue takes millions of dollars a year. In 2007, the world economy slowed down. Governments had less money for environmental projects. Donations to charities that raise money for environmental causes dropped. This looked like bad news for animals and the people committed to protecting them. Fortunately, this dark cloud had a silver lining.

Prior to the poor economy, there was a great construction boom. All over the world, people were buying up land and building houses. Some companies bought huge tracts of unspoiled land hoping to create entire communities. This worried environmental scientists, because habitats were being bulldozed with no regard for the creatures living there. When the economy ground to a halt, people stopped buying new homes. The developers were stuck with land they were willing to sell at any price. Conservation groups sprang into action—they began gobbling up this bargain real estate and making sure it could never be built on again.

Organizations such as the Trust for Public Land bought hundreds of acres at a time. In the future, this property will either be used for parks or recreational space or just be left as wild, open space. Even towns and cities got in on the action, buying space all of their citizens can enjoy. They couldn't resist a bargain either!

ENERGY EFFICIENT

The brightest ideas sometimes come from the environment's darkest days. This provides a ray of hope as we look back at the causes and consequences of the 2010 Gulf oil disaster. Within a year, scientists had a better understanding of what happens to oil when it is spilled into a massive ecosystem such as the Gulf of Mexico. They were able to evaluate the different methods of removing oil from the surface of the water and from the beaches and wetland areas. Their work will help determine how we respond to future oil spills. Doctors, meanwhile, are studying how people are affected by the chemicals used to disperse the oil. They need to understand the short-term and long-term health risks if these chemicals are to be used this way again.

The brightest idea that could come from the Gulf oil disaster—for humans *and* animals—is a new energy plan for the United States. Most everyone agrees that the U.S. needs to find a way to rely less on oil and invest more in clean energy. Other countries need to do this, too. Some have already gotten a good start, while others lag behind. In the U.S., money, politics, and emotions have kept people with different viewpoints from working together on a smart plan. Will the Gulf oil disaster be the wake-up call to finally get serious?

Dueling Do-Gooders

Not all environmentalists think alike. Although environmental groups usually support one another, sometimes they end up going nose to nose over an issue. In 2010, the people planning to build wind turbines in Wyoming, Montana, and Idaho to produce power found themselves fighting a little bird called a sage grouse (below).

The sage grouse is rare. It is also very picky. It won't cross roads, walk under power lines, or lay eggs anywhere near a wind turbine. If the turbines are built, the species could be lost. Green energy supporters and wildlife supporters are at odds over this issue. Fortunately, they are both committed to finding a solution that will work for animals and people.

5 Trailblazers

These people are doing things to help protect endangered species today…and make the world better for tomorrow.

Kirk Johnson

Dentist

Johnson (left) is a dentist in Anchorage, Alaska. When a bald eagle was discovered missing most of its upper beak near his home, Johnson came up with a clever solution. He filled in the missing portion with the same material he uses to fix the teeth of his human patients. The eagle recovered fully and was healthy enough to be released into the wild. Johnson's idea is now being used on species of birds all over the world.

Elizabeth Johnson

Ecologist

Johnson studies the ecosystems in and around New York City, where the effects of habitat loss, pollution, and climate change are especially stressful on animals. She helps people and businesses appreciate their "neighbors"—and even discovered a new species of centipede in Manhattan's Central Park!

Slava Trigubovich

Conservation Biologist

In the years after the break-up of the Soviet Union, the Russian government paid little attention to the health of its vast wilderness areas. As director of a nature reserve in southern Siberia, Trigubovich enlisted the help of local residents to save wildlife in this region. Now he is working with them to protect rare species such as the snow leopard and argali sheep.

Kent Clegg

Farmer

Clegg invented a safe method for catching trumpeter swans near his Idaho farm, where they often crowded a local river. He then moved them to a river 200 miles (322 kilometers) south. There the swans have found more food to eat and more room to live.

6 Field Tested

hen an animal species is reduced to fewer than 50 breeding pairs, it becomes almost impossible to save it from extinction. That does not mean we should stop trying. One of the most successful efforts in this area has been the rebuilding of the California condor population.

The population crashed in the 1980s because of a combination of habitat destruction, pollution, and illegal hunting. Only 22 birds remained when they were captured and bred in two California zoos. The program worked so well that by 1991, several animals were reintroduced into the wild.

Today there are almost 400 California condors. Half are in the wild, while half are still part of the government breeding program. In recent years, visitors to the Grand Canyon in Arizona could hardly believe their eyes. California condors were soaring through the air there, too.

A California condor soars above the Grand Canyon. The tag on its wing was placed there by researchers to track its activity.

7 Career Opportunities
WORKING FOR ANIMALS

F

or young people who care about our relationship with the natural world, there are fascinating jobs on both sides of the Man vs. Animal equation. Scientists, chemists, and engineers are in great demand by companies and governments to work on ideas that benefit humans without hurting animals. These jobs range from designing "green" factories and office buildings to managing emissions and wastewater to testing products in ways that do not hurt living creatures.

Thousands of people begin careers in the green energy field each year. They love animals and care about them. The work they do can benefit thousands of different species. Many people in the fields of solar energy and wind energy, for example, have chosen this kind of work for that very reason. Their mechanical and design skills do the most good helping

A zookeeper checks in on the spider monkeys at the London Zoo in England.

reduce the amount of fossil fuels we use. That, in turn, helps animals threatened by oil drilling and exploration.

There is also great demand for people willing to work in the field of medicine. On any given day, you are likely to read about a doctor or **zoologist** or **anthropologist** who has made an amazing breakthrough. The more we learn about the animal world, the better it will be for all living things. From discovering new species to protecting the ones we already know about, there are few careers more rewarding.

Often the first step toward a career "in the wild" is research. After graduating from high school, many young people volunteer to do research as part of their college courses. The work is hard, and the hours are long, but the information they collect and the remarkable things they see end up in important studies. Many of these students find their life's work during this time. Some go into teaching—they are eager to share what they know with the next generation of enthusiastic students.

College students can have an impact on animals and ecosystems all around the world. That's what happened at the University of Richmond in Virginia. Students in a class on **sustainable** practices wanted to help endangered species in Afghanistan, a country torn apart by war. They compiled a list of animals and presented it to the country's Wildlife Executive Committee. Many animals, including the Egyptian vulture, received protection because of the students' efforts.

Becoming a Zookeeper

To some, no job will do unless they get to be around a wide variety of animals every day. These are the people who become zookeepers. They feed and care for a wide range of animals and also clean up after them. In many zoos, they also take part in studies or research projects. Zookeepers must be very observant and take good notes.

Some zookeepers also give educational talks to visitors. Many young people decide they want to work in a zoo after listening to a zookeeper's presentation. The first step often is to volunteer at a zoo or aquarium to see what the job is all about.

Becoming a zookeeper takes a lot of training. Zookeepers work with animals that used to be wild and can still be dangerous. They must understand the behavior of each animal under their care. They must also learn how to handle these animals in different situations.

Most people who go to work at zoos spend their entire careers there. They wouldn't think of working anywhere else. A few go on to become zoologists. Zoologists are experts in animal biology, behavior, and habitats.

Zookeepers work with animals every day, including species such as elephants that most people rarely come in contact with.

Expert Opinions

When the best minds talk about species at risk, it's worth listening to what they say...

"There is no one 'silver bullet' to end overfishing, because there is no one thing causing overfishing."
—*Mike Crispino, Vice President, Communications & Outreach for the International Seafood Sustainability Foundation, on the difficulty of saving the world's tuna population*

"Probably 99.9 percent of everything you could check off has been impacted...this is Ground Zero."
—*Wayne Keller, Executive Director of the Grand Isle Port Commission, on how many parts of the environment were affected by the 2010 Gulf oil disaster*

"These monsters are challenging the top of the food chain out here, and it's not natural."
—*Ron Bergeron, Fish & Wildlife Conservation Commissioner, on the Burmese pythons that have been set free by their owners in the Florida Everglades*

"If polar bears are going to live to see the next century, we have to rapidly reduce our greenhouse gas emissions and preserve the Arctic, not turn it into a dirty industrial zone."
—*Rebecca Noblin (above), Alaska Director of the Center for Biological Diversity, on saving polar bears from extinction*

"We are trying to re-educate people, who are a big part of the system, about the importance of protecting nature. We are doing this brick by brick—through public meetings, movies, educating children, and so forth."
—*Slava Trigubovich, conservationist, on getting local people to support his nature reserves in Siberia*

"Anything that develops over hundreds of thousands of years deserves a chance to be rescued."
—*Roger Lang, conservationist, on his effort to save a rare species of mountain trout*

9 What Can I Do?

Can there really be a winner when it's humans vs. animals? Yes. The key to victory as you look toward the planet's future is biodiversity. Not every ecosystem has to boast the variety of species of a place such as the Crown of the Continent. But the greater the biodiversity anywhere, the better it is for everyone. That's how nature works best. The most important thing you can do is learn as much as possible about the different species living near your home or school. Once you start looking, you'll be amazed at what you find.

Think of your teachers as partners in this project. Encourage your school to make a biodiversity plan that students can put into action. You can start by making your play areas friendlier to plants and animals. Look for places around the school—maybe even on top of it—where biodiversity projects would work. Think of ways to conserve or restore green spaces.

Finally, it is very likely there are species at risk near where you live. They may even be in your own backyard. Research local conservation groups. For example, Tampa Bay Watch works to protect and restore marine environments and wetlands in the waters of Florida. Like many organizations of this kind, Tampa Bay Watch enlists the support of children and teenagers to help its cause.

Teenagers work on a project by Tampa Bay Watch to create an oyster shell bar.

Glossary

Anthropologist—Someone who studies humans and their evolution.

Biodiversity—The number and variety of plant and animal species in a certain place.

Carbon Dioxide—A colorless gas made up of one part carbon and two parts oxygen.

Climate Change—A long-term change in weather conditions.

Commercial Fishermen—People who fish for a living.

Conservation—The careful preservation and protection of something.

Ecosystems—All the organisms, plants, and animals that make up specific ecological areas.

Emissions—Substances discharged into the air.

Fertilizing—Adding nutrients to soil to help plants grow.

Fungus—An organism that grows on other organisms. Mold and mildew are types of fungus.

Greenhouse Gases—Gases that trap heat in the atmosphere, just as a greenhouse does during the winter.

Human Immunodeficiency Virus (HIV)—A serious medical condition marked by severe weakening of the body's immune system.

Overharvesting—Depleting the population of a species through hunting or fishing.

Parasites—Organisms that live by feeding off of other living things.

Pesticides—Chemicals used to kill bugs that feed on crops.

Plundered—Robbed or taken with great force.

Secrete—Give off.

Sediment—Material that settles at the bottom of something.

Sustainable—Using resources in a way that also helps replenish them.

Zoologist—Someone who studies animals.

Sources

The authors relied on many different books, magazines, and organizations to do research for this book. Listed below are the primary sources of information and their websites:

The Associated Press	www.ap.org
Discover Magazine	www.discovermagazine.com
National Geographic Magazine	ngm.nationalgeographic.com
The New York Times	www.nytimes.com
Newsweek Magazine	www.newsweek.com
Seed Magazine	www.seedmagazine.com
Science Magazine	www.sciencemag.org
Science News	www.sciencenews.org
Time Magazine	www.time.com
U.S. Department of Agriculture	www.usda.gov

Resources

To get involved with efforts to help the environment, you can contact these organizations:

Defenders of Wildlife	www.defenders.org
Earth's Endangered Creatures	www.earthsendangered.com
National Wildlife Federation	www.nwf.org
U.S. Fish & Wildlife Service	www.fws.gov
World Wildlife Fund	www.worldwildlife.org

For more information on the subjects covered in this book:

Harris, John D., and Brown, Paul L., editors. *Wildlife: Destruction, Conservation and Biodiversity.* Happauge, New York. Nova Science Publishers, 2009.

Tait, Malcolm. *Going, Going, Gone? Animals on the Brink of Extinction and How to Turn the Tide.* London, England. Think Books, 2006.

Weston, Chris. *Animals on the Edge: Reporting from the Frontline of Extinction.* London, England. Thames & Hudson, 2009.

Index

Page numbers in **bold** refer to illustrations.

The Authors

AMY K. TILMONT is a science teacher at The Rumson Country Day School in Rumson, New Jersey. She is a graduate of Lycoming College. Her areas of expertise include Geology and Environmental Science.

JEFFREY R. GARSIDE is also a science teacher at The Rumson Country Day School. He graduated from Northeastern University and holds a Masters degree from Kean College. Jeff teaches Chemistry, Physics and Biology, and is head of RCDS's Science Department.

MARK STEWART has written more than 200 non-fiction books for the school and library market. He has an undergraduate degree in History from Duke University. Mark's work in environmental studies includes books on the plants and animals of New York (where he grew up) and New Jersey (where he lives now).